9\15

this or that?

whale

OR

fish?

Susan Kralovansky

Consulting Editor, Diane Craig, M.A./Reading Specialist

Super Sandcastle

An Imprint of Abdo Publishing
www.abdopublishing.com

visit us at www.abdopublishing.com

Published by Abdo Publishing, a division of ABDO, PO Box 398166, Minneapolis, Minnesota 55439. Copyright © 2015 by Abdo Consulting Group, Inc. International copyrights reserved in all countries. No part of this book may be reproduced in any form without written permission from the publisher. Super SandCastle™ is a trademark and logo of Abdo Publishing.

Printed in the United States of America, North Mankato, Minnesota
062014
092014

THIS BOOK CONTAINS
RECYCLED MATERIALS

Editor: Liz Salzmann
Content Developer: Nancy Tuminelly
Cover and Interior Design and Production: Mighty Media, Inc.
Photo Credits: Kelly Doudna, Shutterstock

Library of Congress Cataloging-in-Publication Data
Kralovansky, Susan Holt, author.
 Whale or fish? / Susan Kralovansky ; consulting editor, Diane Craig, M.A., reading specialist.
    pages cm. -- (This or that?)
 Audience: 004-010.
 ISBN 978-1-62403-290-5
 1. Whales--Juvenile literature. 2. Fishes--Juvenile literature. 3. Marine animals--Juvenile literature. I. Craig, Diane, editor. II. Title.
 QL737.C4
 578.77--dc23
                          2013041843

Super SandCastle™ books are created by a team of professional educators, reading specialists, and content developers around five essential components—phonemic awareness, phonics, vocabulary, text comprehension, and fluency—to assist young readers as they develop reading skills and strategies and increase their general knowledge. All books are written, reviewed, and leveled for guided reading, early reading intervention, and Accelerated Reader® programs for use in shared, guided, and independent reading and writing activities to support a balanced approach to literacy instruction.

contents

whale or fish?

Is it a whale? Or is it a fish? Can you tell the difference?

Whales live in the ocean like fish. They swim like fish. They look like fish. But whales are not fish.

Fish come in many shapes, colors, and sizes. Some look like rocks. Others look like worms. Some fish are as flat as pancakes. Others can blow themselves up like balloons.

mammal, not fish

A whale is a mammal. Mammals breathe with **lungs** and are **warm-blooded**. They do not hatch out of eggs. A mother whale feeds her baby milk.

Most fish breathe with **gills**. Most fish are **cold-blooded**. Most fish hatch from eggs. Mother fish do not feed their babies.

skin or scales?

Whales can be black, brown, gray, or white. They have smooth, rubbery skin. Under their skin is a thick **layer** of fat called **blubber**.

Most fish have **tough** skin. Their skin is covered with small plates. The plates are called scales. Fish scales look like **shingles** on a roof.

lungs or gills?

Whales need to come to the surface to breathe. Whales breathe through holes on their heads called blowholes. The air goes from the blowholes to their **lungs**.

Some whales have one blowhole. Others have two.

Most fish do not come to the surface to breathe. They get **oxygen** from the water.

Water goes in through their mouths.
Then it goes out through their **gills**.
The gills take **oxygen** from the water.

flukes or fins?

Whales have two side fins called flippers. They also have tail fins called flukes. A whale moves its flukes up and down to swim.

Fish have body fins. The fins help them keep their balance. Fish tails are called caudal fins. Most fish swim by moving their caudal fins from side to side.

calf or fry?

Baby whales are called calves. Calves are born underwater. The mother pushes her baby to the surface for its first breath. She **protects** her calf from danger.

Baby fish are called fry or fingerlings. Most fish don't take care of their fry after **birth**.

at a glance

whale ———————————— fish

mammal ———————————————— fish

breathes with **lungs** above water —— breathes with **gills** underwater

smooth skin ——————————— skin covered with scales

moves flukes up and down ————— moves caudal fin side to side

babies called calves ——————— babies called fry

a whale of a tale craft

make waves and spout off a cool story about a whale.

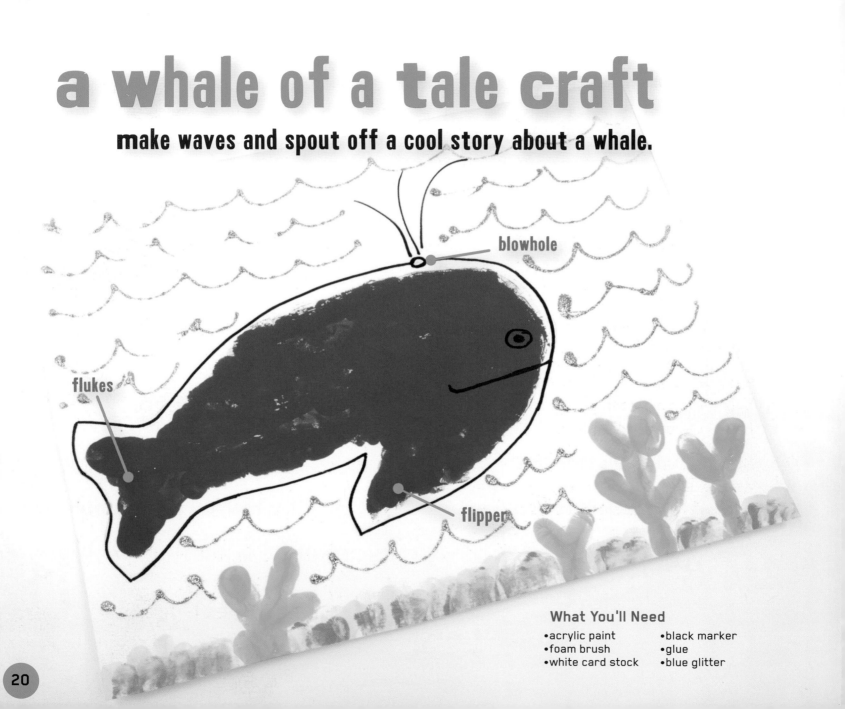

blowhole

flukes

flipper

What You'll Need
- acrylic paint
- foam brush
- white card stock
- black marker
- glue
- blue glitter

Paint your **palm**, fingers, and thumb. Hold your thumb out but keep your fingers together. Make a handprint on the card stock. Dip your finger in paint. Use it to fill in the white spaces. This is your whale's body.

 Dip your finger in paint again. Make two tail flukes at the narrow end of the body.

3 Wash the paint off your hand. Use your fingers to paint the sea floor. Paint sand and plants. Wash your hand each time you change colors. Let the paint dry.

4 Use the marker to outline the whale. Draw a line for the whale's mouth. Draw an eye just above the mouth. Draw a blowhole on the head.

5 Make wavy lines around the whale with glue. Sprinkle blue glitter over the glue lines. Shake off the extra glitter. This is the water. Let the glue dry.

6 Make up a whale of a tale. What is your whale's name? What does it eat? How long can it stay underwater? What kind of adventures does it have?

a fishy story craft

bubble, bubble! this fish goes swimmingly with a great story.

fin

caudal fin

gills

fin

What You'll Need

- acrylic paint
- foam brush
- white card stock
- black marker
- glue
- blue glitter

1. Paint your **palm**, fingers, and thumb. Spread your thumb and pinkie away from your middle three fingers. Make a handprint on the card stock.

2. Wash the paint off your hand. Paint your fingers and thumb a different color. Spread your thumb and pinkie out like before. Make a second handprint a little higher than the first. Dip your finger in the first color of paint. Use it to fill in the middle of your handprint. This is your fish's body.

3. Wash the paint off your hand. Use your fingers to paint the sea floor. Paint sand and plants. Wash your hand each time you change colors. Let the paint dry.

4. Use the marker to outline the fish and draw its mouth. Draw a dot in a circle for the eye. Draw curved lines for the **gills**.

5. Make wavy lines around the fish with glue. Sprinkle blue glitter over the glue lines. Shake off the extra glitter. This is the water. Let the glue dry.

6. Make up a fishy story. What is your fish's name? What does it eat? Where does it live? What kind of adventures does it have?

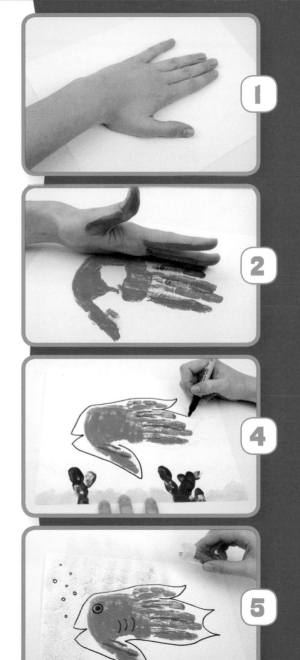

glossary

birth – when a person or animal is born.

cold-blooded – having a body temperature that changes according to the temperature of the surroundings.

gill – the organ on a fish or tadpole's side that it breathes through.

layer – one thickness of something that may be over or under another thickness.

lung – an organ in the body used for breathing air.

oxygen – a colorless gas found in air, water, and most rocks and minerals.

palm – the inside of your hand between your wrist and fingers.

protect – to guard someone or something from harm or danger.

shingle – one of the thin tiles that go on the roof or sides of a building.

tough – strong but flexible.

warm-blooded – having a body temperature that is maintained by the body. It does not change according to the temperature of the surroundings.